Bouquet of Wisdom

Reflections from the Garden

Growing in wisdom—
together!

D

Bouquet of Wisdom
Reflections from the Garden

Deanna Nowadnick

Rhododendron Books
Monroe
Washington

Bouquet of Wisdom
Reflections from the Garden

ISBN: 978-0-9835897-0-9
Library of Congress Control Number: 2022922990

Book Packaging by Tinsy Winsy Studio, BrendaWilbee.com
Interior Art and Layout: Brenda Wilbee
Cover Art and Design: Brenda Wilbee

Printed in the United States of America.

Dedicated to

Phyllis Nowadnick

whose love of flowers and gardening
helped me better appreciate God's love

Other Books by Deanna Nowadnick

Fruit of My Spirit: Reframing Life in God's Grace
Signs in Life: Finding Direction in Our Travels with God

Table of Contents

Introduction

"Blessed is the one who finds wisdom, and the one who gets understanding."

- Proverbs 3:13 (ESV)

On my desk sits a bouquet of roses my husband Kurt picked up at the grocery store. Each one is a different height, a slightly different shade of red. Two stand tall; two are beginning to droop. A faint scent hangs in the air.

Flowers have long been a special part of my day. My father nurtured beautiful red azaleas and Pink Pearl rhododendrons. Every summer Grandma Carstensen lovingly cared for geraniums and begonias. Grandma Thorp carefully snipped purple pansies for backyard tea parties. And years later I would spend evenings with a trowel and clippers, tending my own perennial collection of lacy cornflowers, golden daylilies, fragrant phlox, and towering lupines.

For me, flowers speak the language of love, not only Kurt's love and my family's love of gardening, but God's love for all of us. I see his love in his creativity, his attention to detail, his provision. Some flowers thrive in the sun; others want shade. All are beautiful creations unique in color and design. And isn't that also true for us?

Bouquet of Wisdom is a thirty-day devotional of personal stories, each one paired with a flower and a lesson. I look back on a little girl who found courage in a bouquet of sticky dandelions. I remember the teenager who wilted in the spotlight of a daffodil pageant. I treasure Christmas memories that include poinsettias in a hospital, paperwhites sitting on rocks, and beautiful blue hydrangeas in Brazil. Some blossoms remind me of God's faithfulness; others emphasize his care. Each experience was a lesson learned—in season and out of season, in the garden and in my life.

Perhaps flowers have meant something to you, too. Not only are they lovely, but they can connect us to times of transition, celebration, and even challenge. Do wild flowers remind you of the wild child within? Does a prom corsage bring back memories of a special dance, a first date, a certain young man? Does a particular flower remind you of God's provision? Maybe it's a garden favorite that survived a brutally cold winter, the hottest July, and last week's hail storm.

In life's memorable blossoms is a God who's been in the details of our life. And in those experiences, he helps us find wisdom and gain understanding—not conventional wisdom, but divinely inspired, discerning insight. Yes, the flowers surrounding us create a unique collection of memories, and those memories can become an exquisite bouquet of wisdom and understanding.

My bouquet begins with those sticky dandelions and that lesson in courage.

"Where will we get flowers?"

Dandelions and Courage

"for God gave us a spirit not of fear but of power and love and self-control."

- 2 Timothy 1:7 (ESV)

The vacant lot at the end of my street was the stage for many childhood adventures, but rarely did I venture from the footpath that meandered through it. I was convinced the tall grass hid ginormous, slithering snakes. If friends were hunting for buried treasure, I found a reason to dig where I stood. If sailing the seven seas, I volunteered to stay "on ship."

One day in second grade while walking home from school, I left the path. School was five blocks from home, only four if I cut through the vacant lot, a perfect shortcut as long as I stayed on the beaten path. Sally, a classmate and neighborhood friend, often walked with me. Not only did we have matching brown and tan saddle shoes, but on this particular afternoon we also had matching construction paper baskets, an art project for May Day bouquets.

"Where will we get flowers?" I asked Sally.

Before she could answer, we turned the corner—and saw them! Beautiful yellow dandelions in the tall grass of the vacant lot. Sally ran ahead, but I froze, fearing those snakes. My shoulders sagged. If I was going to have my own bouquet, I'd need to leave the path.

I took a step, one small step into the monstrously scary grass. I looked down for signs of critterly movement. My breath caught. After a cautious second step, weeds brushed my bare legs. I shivered in apprehension. I looked back, then ahead. Surrounded now by the high grass, I took a third step that put me close enough to stretch out and grab the flowers. One handful of sticky-stemmed dandelions, some short, others long, stems torn as quickly as possible and tucked into my basket.

I had my flowers.

Until then, absolutely nothing had gotten me off the trail, whether hurrying home from school or sailing the seven seas. My fear of huge, slithering snakes had stopped me in my tracks. But that afternoon, I stepped out for a bouquet of flowers.

In a letter to a follower, the apostle Paul tells Timothy we are given a spirit of power, love, and self-control, not fear. In second grade I found power for that first step, courage for a scary time. Love for my mother propelled me to take a second step, feelings that transcended my hesitancy. Self-control guided all my steps and gave me strength for a sticky situation, keeping panic at bay.

Do you ever hesitate when leaving life's beaten path for something you want or need? Fear of the unknown can still stop me. In life's tall grass, I can find myself fretting about ginormous things that might be lurking and slithering in ways that might scare me. Perhaps you do too, but God walks with us. We don't have to be afraid. We can take steps, because we are given power, love, and self-control.

The dandelion's yellow color can be associated with fear and cowardice. Not for me. I see yellow dandelions and remember a courageous little girl who didn't let fear stop her.

> *Heavenly Father, give us courage for those times when we are uncertain, even scared. Help us find our power, love, and self-control in you so we don't have to be fearful. We can take steps. Amen.*

Digging Deeper

Any childhood fears that stopped you in your tracks?

When has fear kept you from something you've wanted or needed?

How has God helped you to take steps when you've had to leave the "beaten path"?

"Um... Um... Um..."

2 Daffodils in the Spotlight

"for all have sinned and fall short of the glory of God, and are justified by his grace as a gift, through the redemption that is in Christ Jesus."

- Romans 3:23-24 (ESV)

I was ecstatic! Over the school intercom, I heard my name. I was a finalist for Daffodil Princess! For the upcoming festivities, I would need a dress, shoes, nail polish, and makeup, along with an appointment for a haircut. I'd also need to memorize a five-minute speech. Teachers were going to judge us on our appearance as well as our poise and speaking ability.

By the big night, I was ready. I had the perfect navy blue, knee-length, lacy crepe dress and matching shoes, blue eyeshadow and red nail polish. My hair was perfectly styled. I planned to talk about my grandfather's emigration from Germany, his journey through Ellis Island, his new life farming in Eastern Washington, his pride and determination, his love of family. It was going to be perfect.

It was not perfect.

On stage, in the bright lights, I forgot my lines—three times. My face scrunched in concentration. My mouth twisted trying to find words. My hands flailed in distress. Finally, cheeks burning, knees shaking, I adlibbed a grand finale, but it was not grand.

I was not named Daffodil Princess. I did not leave the stage with a bouquet of spring color. Despite my "perfect" preparations, I'd faltered. My excitement overtook me; my onstage debut overwhelmed me. One stumble led to another. That stumble led to more, all coming in front of family and friends, my prom date, everyone from English class, and my annoying younger brother.

My stumbles were painful, not just for me but for everyone. Mom and Dad saw it all. They knew how hard I'd prepared, the care and attention I'd given to every detail. Driving home, I don't remember what they said; I just remember being surrounded by love and support and feelings of encouragement. Even my annoying younger brother was a little less annoying.

The apostle Paul talks about perfection in a letter to the Romans. He explains how we all fall short of God's glory, his expectations, his "appearance, poise, and speaking" criteria. However, Paul goes on to say that we are made right by God's grace, his unmerited love and forgiveness, his support and encouragement.

My high school yearbook devotes two pages to the crowning of the Daffodil Princess. The winner had "put her best foot forward," not something I'd been able to do. Even with my "perfect" preparations, I'd fallen short. On those same yearbook pages my name is also misspelled. It's like it wasn't really me. At least it wasn't who I wanted to be.

We all try to put our best foot forward, but we all fall short of God's glory. We stumble—again and again and again. And when we do, God offers his grace.

Even after miserable nights in the bright lights.

Loving, merciful God, we have all sinned and fallen short of your glory again and again. Surround us with the gift of your grace. Comfort us with your love and forgiveness. Amen.

Digging Deeper

Have you had a memorable "on stage" experience?

Any "perfect" preparations that were not perfect?

Knowing God makes us right with him when we fall short, how does this help you when facing challenges? Embracing opportunities?

"It's Vincent van Gogh!"

Ordinary Sunflowers

"The LORD looks down from heaven; he sees all the children of man."

- Psalm 33:13 (ESV)

I first became fascinated with Vincent van Gogh while watching my father paint his own version of the grand master's "Sunflowers." I became passionate about van Gogh while standing in front of his "Starry Night" at the Museum of Modern Art in New York City. Nothing could have prepared me for my feelings of awe and wonder. The painting enchanted me, pulling me close, pushing me back. At one point I leaned precariously over the ropes that outlined the designated viewing area and heard the guard caution, "Ma'am, I need you to step back."

I tipped my head to the side, smiled, and shrugged. "I'm so sorry! It's Vincent van Gogh!"

Not only did the boldness of the artist's night scene entrance me, but his smaller brushstrokes beckoned me closer. Dramatic circles of color surrounded his moon and stars, but my attention kept returning to the short lines of yellow and orange used to create windows in the painting's village. Up close his simple lines of color looked like carelessly applied globs of paint. But stepping back—as I'd been directed to do—I could actually make out a villager in one of the windows.

I caught myself glancing back when I finally walked away. Who was the villager in the window? Did he ever see himself in van Gogh's finished work? It would have been impossible for him to imagine his eventual place in art history. Even if told, he might have said, "I'm just a potato farmer." He might have shuffled his feet and said, "I was just looking out the window one night." Yes, he would have been astounded to learn of his eventual place in van Gogh's extraordinary artwork, a single stroke of color in a grand master's grand collection.

At times I've not appreciated my own stroke of color in our Grand Master's collection, using "just" to describe my own circumstances: I'm *just* working part-time; I'm *just* a volunteer; I'm *just* learning. Have you made similar comments? Felt the same? Like van Gogh's villager, it's hard to fathom our ordinariness as part of something eternally extraordinary.

Yet the Bible includes scores of ordinary women who become part of God's extraordinary story. Some are named; many are not. If asked, they too might have replied, "I'm just…" Rahab might have said, "I'm just helping a couple spies." Ruth might have answered, "I'm just taking my mother-in-law home." Dorcas might have said, "I'm just sewing for the poor." All would have been surprised by their place in the biggest story ever told.

Describing "Sunflowers" in an 1889 letter to his brother Theo, van Gogh said, "It's a type of painting that changes its aspect a little, which grows in richness the more you look at it." God's extraordinary story of love and faithfulness also changes its aspect the more we look at our very ordinary place in his window. Up close, our life might look like globs of paint, but stepping back there's a richness I'm "just" now learning to appreciate. You too?

God of all creation, you look down from heaven and see us. You include our ordinariness as part of your extraordinary. Help us appreciate our place in your great masterpiece. Amen.

Digging Deeper

Is there an artist who fascinates you? Who pulls you close?

Where have you used the word “just” to describe yourself?

What title would God put on your “ordinary” place in his extraordinary masterpiece?

"Does this mean we're not going to Brazil?"

4 Poinsettias and Expectations

"For to us a child is born, to us a son is given; and the government will be on his shoulder, and his name shall be called Wonderful Counselor, Mighty God, Everlasting Father, Prince of Peace."

- Isaiah 9:6 (ESV)

Three years after our son Kevin married Manoela, a beautiful young woman from Brazil, we began planning a Christmas trip to her home country. Our travels were going to take us from one continent to another over nine countries and through six time zones. I was anxious to get our arrangements in place, but when I asked Kevin about plane tickets, he put me off, "Mom, I'm watching airfares—"

"Son, I don't need to save another $10 each way. Can we go ahead and book our flights?"

At this point, Kevin suggested we all meet for dinner, so Kurt and I joined Kevin and Manoela at a favorite Italian restaurant. Our older son, Kyle, and his wife, Katie, came along too. After sitting down, Manoela smiled and handed me a small box. "A little something for Christmas," she said.

Inside was the sonogram for our first grandchild! But still focused on our upcoming trip, I blurted out, "Oh! Does this mean we're not going to Brazil?"

"Mom," Kyle interjected, "you might want to try that again. Perhaps an 'Oh! How exciting!'"

Yes, very exciting! Six months later Enzo was born on Christmas Day. Rather than navigate airport concourses, we got to navigate hospital corridors. Holding him for the first time, I marveled at the precious little boy in my arms. We'd awaited the birth of "a" baby with great excitement, never imagining the birth of "this" baby.

Dearest Enzo, a gift so much greater than we ever expected.

Two thousand years before Enzo's birth, an angel appeared to Mary. Just as Manoela had reached out with her announcement, the angel reached out with the announcement of God's love and the promise of a baby. No sonogram here. No flights put on hold. No "We're not going to Brazil?" outburst. Just the fulfillment of Isaiah's Old Testament prophesy: A child would be born, a son given. A baby who would be called Wonderful Counselor, Almighty God, Prince of Peace, Everlasting Father.

The night of Enzo's birth, we walked through a hospital decorated with poinsettias. Their star-shaped leaves have come to symbolize the star above Bethlehem, their scarlet color representative of the blood Jesus shed on the cross. In a small bassinet, we found our promised grandchild, the long awaited and greatly anticipated addition to our family. Away in a manger, we found our promised Savior, our long awaited and greatly anticipated Messiah, a gift greater than all our expectations!

> *Glorious God in the highest heaven, you gave us a baby greater than all our expectations! Away in a manger you gave us a Savior who would be named Wonderful Counselor, Mighty God, Everlasting Father, Prince of Peace. Amen.*

Digging Deeper

When has a major disappointment become an unexpected blessing?

Describe a gift that exceeded your expectations.

Isaiah's prophesy announced the birth of a child who would be called Wonderful Counselor, Mighty God, Everlasting Father, Prince of Peace. How do these names help you better understand who the baby would be?

"Black tar?"

5

Hedge Roses and Hearts of Tar

"And I will give them one heart, and a new spirit I will put within them..."

- Ezekiel 11:19 (ESV)

I have an adult tricycle I peddle about my neighborhood. It's pink and has a basket and a bell. I wave at other bikers, call out to people walking, and ring my bell for small children who usually giggle. Some days I go for coffee; other days I bike around a small lake. Sometimes I run errands or meet friends. But every day I marvel at blooming flowers, freshly mown grass, and seasonal changes to the trees.

A favorite place on my ride is a home with a hedge of pink roses along the sidewalk. During the summer, the roses are strikingly beautiful. In the fall, I watch as someone carefully prunes and mulches them. Every spring I wait for the leaves to return, the stems to grow tall. And then one day I'll start down the street and see them! Buds that have popped open in the morning sun, blooms of a delicate pink so profuse I can barely see the leaves on the stems.

Nearing the flowers one warm summer day, I glanced down at the asphalt beneath my tires and noticed a heart of tar in the pavement. I'd passed the spot many times before, but I'd always been focused on the roses. Looking closer, I saw how road repairs had been finished with cordiform sealant in the shape of a heart, three feet by four feet. A broken place in the road had been smoothed over, made new, and then framed with a black heart, a beautiful black heart.

Biking home, I thought about the beautiful parts of God's creation. I love pink hedge roses. I also love the beautiful parts of my faith: church celebrations, music that lifts my spirits, sermons that wow me. But the discovery of the heart made me think about a not-so-beautiful part of my faith—my own brokenness. Like a road needing repairs, my sins are rough places badly in need of repair, potholes needing to be made right. Jesus' death on a cross mends my brokenness and covers my sinfulness. With his love, I am made new.

A heart of tar had been part of a long, difficult afternoon of repairs for a road crew. My forgiveness and renewal were part of a long, difficult afternoon of suffering for my Savior. And now I feel like I'm surrounded by God's version of a heart of tar: repaired, made new, and sealed with love.

Yes, there are lots of beautiful flowers to behold, but I've learned there are also hearts of tar in the roads throughout my neighborhood. I look for them now. They're beautiful black reminders of God's love. Any in your neighborhood?

Dearest Jesus, our Savior and Redeemer, we humbly thank you for fixing our brokenness with your own pain and suffering on the cross. Your Spirit surrounds us with love and seals us with grace. Amen.

Where have you seen hearts of tar in your neighborhood?

Describe the beautiful and the not-so-beautiful parts of your faith.

Where in life's brokenness has God surrounded you with a heart of tar?

"If it's to be, it's up to me!"

Fruity Viburnum

"But the fruit of the Spirit is love, joy, peace, patience..."
- Galatians 5:22 (ESV)

I looked up from my crossword. "Kurt, today the garage door wouldn't open. I got stuck outside after my morning walk."

"It's probably the battery in the keypad."

I could see he was headed out to take care of the problem. I glanced at my watch. "We don't need to fix it tonight."

"It'll just take a minute."

I was tired, but before I could object, Kurt was on his way to the garage. I should have been grateful. I often leave the house without my keys, using the garage door's keypad to get inside. Kurt had suggested hiding a key outside just in case, but I'd ignored him and now I was feeling impatient and unappreciative of Kurt's willingness to help when I had no energy for a small home maintenance project. Still, I got up and followed him.

While I held the flashlight, Kurt probed slots and crevices with a screwdriver, trying to find his way into the opener's battery compartment. When he left to find a different screwdriver, I started pulling at the face cover, twisting the top, prying the bottom. I thought a good tug would surely pop the top

Unsuccessful, I went back into the house. I wanted an answer—now, right now—so I sat down at my computer and began an internet search: *How do I change the battery in my garage door's keypad?* Up popped a video with instructions for *sliding* the cover to access the battery.

A simple slide of the cover! No tools necessary! Thirty-four minutes into our “it’ll just take a minute” project, we had a new battery installed and a garage door that opened and closed. I also had a disturbing realization: My very impatient “if it’s to be, it’s up to me” pout and shrug, agitation and frustration had obscured Kurt’s care and concern.

I’ve also had that same uncomfortable realization in my interactions with God. Too often, I’ll heave a “Dear God” sigh and look for my own solutions—now, right now. My impatience surfaces with an attitude, my own tools, and even an internet search, blinding me to God’s care and concern in the small repairs to my dysfunctional outlook.

In Galatians Paul names nine fruits of God’s Spirit, beginning with love, joy, peace, and patience. While changing the battery, my *impatience* impacted my entire spirit. I may have done what needed to be done, but that dead battery robbed me of some love, a little joy, a battery’s worth of peace and patience, and a lot of gratitude for my husband’s care and concern.

After replacing the battery, Kurt hid a spare house key in a container under the viburnum in our backyard. This Pacific Northwest shrub is covered with small white flowers each spring. Blue berries follow late summer. The plant is not particularly noteworthy, but Kurt’s gesture was. Inside the container was not only a key but also a lesson in the fruit of God’s Spirit for the wife who needed it.

Heavenly Father, help us be grateful for the care and concern of others. May our actions and our attitudes honor your Spirit and reflect your fruit. Amen.

Digging Deeper

Have you had an impatient "if it's to be, it's up to me" pout and shrug? What happened?

Knowing impatience can impact our entire spirit, how can you keep a small incident from becoming a bigger one?

Where do you see God's fruit in your life?

Love

Joy

Peace

Patience

The Never Ready, Joyous Noise
Backup Band and Chorale Ensemble

7 Lilies and the Seasons

"For everything there is a season, and a time for every matter under heaven."

- Ecclesiastes 3:1 (ESV)

During the 2020 pandemic, our church streamed its worship services online. For Easter, Pastor Todd asked that I record a violin solo. I picked a favorite Keith and Kristyn Getty hymn, "The Power of the Cross." I practiced and practiced, but when I went to record, my performance was not powerful. I assumed the acoustics were bad and moved from one room to another. The second recording was also not powerful. I thought my computer might be the problem, so I filmed with my camera.

Watching the third recording, I was startled. Without a keyboard and singers to accompany me, my intonation was not pitch-perfect. I was also able to see how arthritis was hampering my posture, the way in which I held my violin and bow. For years, I'd wondered when my playing days might be over. My recordings seemed to suggest the time was now.

After putting my instrument back into its case, perhaps for the last time, I began to reflect on various memories: the fifth-grade talent show, a junior high orchestra concert, the Christmas I played "Silent Night" in memory of Dad, the New Year's Eve service when I tackled a portion of Handel's "Messiah." I found myself feeling grateful, honored to have been a musician, delighted God had found ministry opportunities for me and my violin in so many different places at so many different times.

If I could, I'd hang onto the summer months of my life as a violin player, but winter had come. And the coldness of that reality is not easy, knowing there's not going to be another spring in which to play. I loved the violin. I loved old hymns, contemporary worship songs, even those arrangements with every last note played on the off-beat. I groaned when our bass player heckled me about having to play in the key of A with three sharps. I laughed when he tagged us the "Never Ready Joyous Noise Backup Band and Chorale Ensemble."

A well-known verse from Ecclesiastes reminds us there is a season for everything. A time to be born and a time to die. A time to plant and a time to harvest. A time to grieve and a time to dance. A time to play the violin and a time to serve in other ways.

When our boys were small, I did not accompany the bass player on Sunday mornings; I was busy enough trying to get us all into a pew by ten o'clock. During that particular season in life, I served behind the scenes. Later, when our church was between pastors, I helped with office tasks, something I'd done in an earlier season as a teenager. And now after years of playing my violin, I could look forward to helping during worship, even greeting people at the door on Sunday.

Beautiful white lilies are a seasonal treat. At Easter they decorate our church. After the holiday, they're often planted in a garden by the front entry. Each spring I watch as delicate green shoots poke through the soil. They always make me smile. Also planted in my memories are the green shoots of my own Easters past. Playing my violin was a blessing, a truly wonderful season, one that will always make me smile. God says there is a time for everything, a promise filling me with joy and anticipation, because it's now a new season.

Heavenly Father, we thank you for leading us through our seasons of service. Help us remember there is a season for everything. Amen.

Describe ways in which you're serving now.

How has your service changed over the years?

After your service ended in particular area, how did God lead you to something new?

"Oh, God! No, God!"

8 Orchids and Rough Seas

"Let your eyes look straight ahead; fix your gaze directly before you."

- Proverbs 4:25 (NIV)

Kurt and I traveled with our family to Kauai for our daughter-in-law Katie's 30th birthday. Our week included an ocean cruise along the Na Pali Coast. The sales brochure promised four hours where "the afternoon sun brings a special magical hue to the majestic Na Pali Coast."

Except when it doesn't.

I barely glimpsed the Na Pali Coast. I don't remember magical hues. I spent the entire time holding my stomach. In the sales brochure of beautiful photos, I'd overlooked the words, "Come prepared for the beauty, the motion, and the ocean." More accurately stated? ***The motion of the ocean.***

Ninety minutes into a four-hour adventure our sixty-foot catamaran, The Lucky Lady, turned north into turbulent seas. Through the static of the boat's intercom system, the captain announced, "Friends, welcome aboard. As you can see ***and feel***, we've encountered some choppy water. Please be seated for the next ten minutes."

But instead of ten minutes of choppy waters, we encountered ninety minutes of ten-foot swells. I don't do ten-foot swells. I grabbed the railing and groaned, "Oh, God. No, God." Waves of nausea swept over me. Frantic, I looked around for calm, but a sixty-foot boat battling high seas has no calm.

At our turnaround point in the cruise, the captain stopped the boat for photos. Our backdrop was stunning, but I could only force a smile. *Now can we go home?* Seeing my misery, knowing we had another ninety-minutes of sailing, Kyle counseled, "Mom, keep your eyes on the shore. You gotta stay focused on something."

In Proverbs we find practical advice for choppy times, not on a catamaran, but in life. We are encouraged to look straight ahead, to fix our gaze directly before us, not on a shoreline, but on God. Life is turbulent. We reel and stumble, lose our bearings, and feel absolutely miserable. Perhaps it's a lost job, a lost relationship, a lost friendship. Perhaps it's a serious health concern. Maybe we've just run out of patience with the boss.

At one point in our return trip, I shut my eyes while the boat crashed through more waves and even higher seas. Taking a peek during a very short lull, I looked across the boat and saw Kyle pointing to his eyes. "Focus, Mom."

When we close our eyes to what's happening, the situation doesn't just go away. I had three hours of misery on our cruise. Working through life's turbulence can take days and weeks, even years. We might stagger in frustration, despair, or grief. But when we focus on God, when we fix our gaze on him, he steadies us.

Kurt never left my side on the boat, even holding my just-in-case (but thankfully not necessary) bucket. In life, God never leaves our side either. And should he find us with our eyes squeezed tightly shut during turbulence, he will find a way to get our attention, like Kyle did for me. We might even hear him whisper, "Focus."

We celebrated Katie's birthday at a luau the night following our cruise, each of us adorned with a lei of beautiful orchids. I enjoyed their magical hue, happy to focus on the calm, dry land of the pineapple estate.

> *Father in heaven, help us keep our eyes on you when life gets turbulent. Help us stay focused wherever we might be, wherever we might go. Amen.*

Digging Deeper

When have you found yourself in choppy waters? Where were you?

During life's turbulence, how have you been able to keep your focus on God?

How has refocusing on God helped you find calm? Stay calm?

"Really? You'd do it?"

Ocotillos and Faith

"Now faith is confidence in what we hope for and assurance about what we do not see."

- Hebrews 11:1 (NIV)

"Really? You'd do it?" I asked Kurt incredulously. We were standing on the west rim of the Grand Canyon, looking toward the Skywalk, a modern marvel of cantilevered glass and steel that extended out over the Colorado River far below.

Really. He'd do it. Kurt was willing to take a 68-foot walk on a glass deck above the mile-high canyon, nothing but blue sky surrounding him. Not wanting to be left behind, not wanting fear to rule my decision, I replied with more confidence than I really felt, "Then I'll do it too!"

Together we approached the Skywalk. I gripped the side rail at the entrance and stepped slowly and cautiously onto the walkway, careful to stay on the narrow edging where the glass was opaque. I did not look down. I did not step with confidence. My knees shook. My hands got clammy. My eyes watered. At some point I noticed the view—not the view down into the canyon, but the view out over the canyon, and for a few brief seconds, I marveled at the beautiful rock walls, the majesty of God's grand design, the desert cacti blooming next to tumbleweeds.

According to signs, the Skywalk had been designed to withstand "seismic shifts" and "wind forces" and built to hold the weight of seventy fully loaded 747 passenger jets. *Fully loaded passenger jets?* Important information, but standing on the glass deck, the vertical drop taking my breath away, it didn't matter. The view frightened me. A fall breeze felt like a gale force wind, not because the walkway moved, but because I feared it might. I had to have confidence in the Skywalk's design and construction. Still, my steps were tentative; my heart raced. I never looked down through the glass floor. I had to have faith.

Paul describes faith in Hebrews as confidence in what we hope for and assurance in what we do not see. I need that kind of faith. Whether stepping *onto* a glass walkway or *into* days of uncertainty, faith stabilizes seismic shifts and steadies us all in gale-force winds—whether buffeted by family concerns or job snags, short-term inconveniences or long-term dilemmas, the loss of a loved one, or the loss of direction.

Faith allows me to say "I'll get through this," and mean it. Without faith, my heart races. I'm weak-kneed and unable to move forward. I'm stuck in fear and uncertainty, second-guessing every decision. With faith, I'm able to take a step with confidence and assurance.

Outside the entrance to the Skywalk are ocotillos, a desert succulent with long spindly branches rising from the ground. Crimson flame-shaped flowers bloom on the tips of individual stems, like fourth of July sparklers. The gift shop sold dried branches as walking sticks, a thoughtful reminder for those of us looking for confidence when taking tentative steps.

Father in heaven, give us confidence in what we hope for. Give us assurance about what we do not see. Give us faith. Amen.

Describe a scary situation that took your breath away.

When have you had more determination than courage?

How has faith enabled you to take the next step when uncertain?

"Look at me! Look at me!"

10

Snowdrops "Seen and Heard"

"You have searched me, LORD, and you know me. You know when I sit and when I rise; you perceive my thoughts from afar. You discern my going out and my lying down; you are familiar with all my ways."

- Psalm 139:1-3 (NIV)

During a January visit to New York City, I convinced Kurt to be part of NBC's "Window on the Street" crowd for their morning *Today Show*. During the live taping, we would stand outside Studio 1A on 48th Street and watch the anchors and their guests through the windows. In the icy 17 degrees, I'm sure Kurt could think of a better way to end our week in the city, but he gallantly agreed.

We left our hotel near Central Park on the day of the show and walked ten brutally cold blocks in early morning darkness. At 6:30 a.m., we were cleared by security and allowed to find our place outside the studio. At 7:00, when the show started, we were peering in the windows. Every part of me wanted to jump up and down, wave and yell, "Look at me! Look at me!" And then they did! During a commercial break, Andrea Mitchell, NBC's Chief Foreign Affairs Correspondent, winked at me from inside the studio. I winked back. During a longer break, the anchors came outside to the plaza and greeted the small crowd of freezing fans. Al Roker shook my hand. Craig Melvin smiled from across the plaza. I smiled and waved back. And then my favorite, Hoda Kotb, gave me a wink, a smile, and a wave! I mouthed the words, "I love you!"

My spirits soared. I stood taller, my shoulders back, my head up. I was delighted. I'd been seen by my *Today Show* people.

God sees us too—not because we're standing in just the right spot at just the right time, like I was in New York City, but because he knows us and knows where we are and where we'll be. He even comes out of his heavenly studio, so to speak, to be with us on the street, sending his only Son to walk with us and talk with us, to save us from the outtakes of any given day. The *Today Show* people gave me a wink, a nod, and a wave. God gives us love and support, mercy and grace.

When we got back from our trip, I found perennial snowdrops bursting into bloom in a frozen side garden. Their small blossoms are one of the earliest signs of spring. The plants are only about four inches tall and like their name suggests, they look like delicate white snowflakes. The winter blooms punctuate the end of one season and announce the start to another. In their own way, they call, "Look at me! Look at me!" I'm always delighted to see them. My spirits always soar.

God sees. From heaven, he sees. From a sidewalk and a plaza, he sees. God knows when we sit and when we stand, when we come and when we go. And every part of me wants to jump up and down, wave and yell, "You see me! You see me!"

> *Great God in heaven, you know us, when we sit and when we rise, when we come and go. You know our thoughts. You know our ways. Thank you for seeing each one us. Amen.*

Digging Deeper

Any delightfully close encounters with people you've admired?

Can you think of a time when you really needed to be seen? Describe the circumstances.

How has God helped you to feel "seen and heard" in the plazas of your own life?

"My will be done…"

11 Hydrangeas and Dreams

"The heart of man plans his way, but the LORD establishes his steps."

- Proverbs 16:9 (ESV)

Kevin married Manoela on a fishing dock with Elliott Bay and the city of Seattle their backdrop. Kurt and I traveled to her home country five years later for our long-awaited Christmas trip to Brazil with the Atlantic Ocean and coastal community of Imbituba *our* backdrop. Sitting outside our cottage, I marveled at the view: the rugged coastline, the exotic flowers, geckos darting here and there. My laptop in front of me, I prepared to write and reflect on our international adventures, the joy of meeting my daughter-in-law's extended family, and the excitement of Christmas in another land.

And there it was! The dream I'd had for years, a vision in which I'm sitting outside and writing, water in front of me, red-tiled roofs surrounding me. I imagined being on the west coast of Italy by the Mediterranean Sea, the red-tiled roofs of Cinque Terre all around. But here I was on the east coast of Brazil by the Atlantic Ocean, the red-tiled roofs of our resort around me. I sat and stared, overcome with emotion. My breath caught. Tears slipped down my cheeks. My dream of Italy had become a reality in Brazil.

I'm a dreamer. Some of my dreams include exciting possibilities, like writing in a faraway land, but some of my dreams are very specific prayers in which I provide God with dates, times, and places. I'll even suggest how. And when that happens, my prayers become a "my will be done" to-do list for God long before I say "Amen."

When his disciples asked about prayer, Jesus said to pray like this: "Our Father in heaven, hallowed be your name. Your kingdom come, your will be done, on earth as it is in heaven" (Matthew 6:9-10). *God's* will be done, not mine.

My dreams are important to God. He loves that I think about writing and travel. It's how he created me. Your dreams are important too. He loves when we aspire, when we imagine the possibilities. But we're reminded to wait on God for his guidance and timing. Wise King Solomon said, "The heart of man plans his way, but the Lord establishes his steps." We plan, but God directs. And whether traveling or navigating life's challenges, God surprises and delights us in ways not expected, like he did for me in Brazil.

Hydrangeas bloomed during our time in southern Brazil. Flowering shrubs with globes of light blue, dark blue, pink, and purple lined the highways and side roads. Hydrangeas also surrounded me in Imbituba. I delighted in the lush, luxuriant blossoms. Not only had my dream become real, but it had become real in a way I never imagined.

I'd focused on Italy, not realizing my dream might become a reality in Brazil. I envisioned a sun setting over the Mediterranean, never imagining a sun rising over the Atlantic. My heart planned, but the Lord directed my steps.

Our Father in heaven, you know our hearts. You know our dreams, our plans for the future. Direct our steps this day and always. Amen.

Digging Deeper

Any dreams that became real in an unexpected way?

How has God's reality been even more beautiful than your dreams?

How do your prayers change when thinking about God's will in your life, not just when traveling on holiday, but when navigating life's challenges or unexpected opportunities.

"What about empathy?"

12 Dahlias and Empathy

"Rejoice with those who rejoice, weep with those who weep."

- Romans 12:15 (ESV)

At the end of a coffee date with my friend Michol, she asked, "So, Deanna, what have you learned these past many weeks?"

I set my coffee down, thinking about the drudgery. I'd been cramming for an investment law exam, working my way through a 709-page study guide.

"Michol, I've learned the finer points of security law. I know the difference between state and federal rules and regulations. I can calculate the standard deviation of five numbers, the future value of an investment, and arithmetic mean. I know the difference between calls and puts, market and limit orders, whole and variable life insurance products."

Michol took a long, slow sip of her non-fat, sugar-free vanilla latte. "What about empathy?"

Empathy? I started to laugh.

"No, I'm serious," she said. "What about empathy? When you think about all the work you've been doing, are there any bigger lessons learned?"

I needed to get back to my studies, but promised to think about how empathy might be one of my lessons learned.

At my desk, I opened to Chapter 9 of my study guide and began reviewing the intricacies of investment law at the state level. I plowed through sample math problems in quantitative analysis. I took another practice quiz "where P = Current Price of Bond, N = Number of Periods until Call, and C = Coupon…" My head hurt. My eyes ached. I was tired and irritable. *Empathy*?

For two long months—nine grueling weeks—I'd been studying day after day, hour after hour. I started #MindNumbingMonday posts on Facebook, sharing tediously wearisome concepts from various chapters and quizzes. I took walks. I took naps. *Empathy*?

Unable to shake Michol's question, I thought about how she'd taken time from her own busy schedule to visit. And then I saw the answer to her question. Studying the difference between calls and puts had not invoked empathy on *my* part, but it had helped me appreciate empathy on *her* part. My dear *empathetic* friend had shared not just coffee with me, but she'd also given me some much-needed respite at a time when I was feeling overwhelmed.

The apostle Paul tells us in Romans to rejoice with those who rejoice and weep with those who weep. Michol had "wept" with me that day over coffee. She'd also challenged me. I think she was hoping I'd learn empathy from my drudgery, my own frustration and pain, but I actually saw it in her kindness. Empathy didn't come from what I was doing; it came from what she was doing.

A couple weeks after my exam, I found a bouquet of colorful dahlias at my front door. Another friend and her two young sons had left the surprise. Every flower was a different color—shades of red and yellow, a variegated purple—each one unique in size and shape, all coming together beautifully in a small plastic cup of water. I smiled, thinking about my empathetic friends, one who'd taken time to encourage me, another who'd taken time to rejoice with me. *Yes, empathy.*

Lord Jesus, help us grow in empathy so we can rejoice with those who rejoice and weep with those who weep. Amen.

Who has been there with empathy in your life? What was the occasion?

How have you been able to "weep with those who weep"? Where have you been able to "rejoice with those who rejoice"?

Why does God want us to "rejoice with those who rejoice, weep with those who weep"?

"Wonderful times! Great memories!"

13 Azaleas and Thinking of Home

"This is the day that the LORD has made; let us rejoice and be glad in it."

- Psalm 118:24 (ESV)

Manoela asked me about our family's videos. "I want to see Kevin when he was a little boy, to hear his voice, his giggle."

I looked inside the family room closet. Where to begin? Twenty-five years of yet-to-be-organized memories gathered dust on the shelf. Since we were all about to leave on a family vacation, I thought we could bring a tape or two, so I asked Kurt to pick a couple from when the boys were little. Watching him grab cassette after cassette after cassette, I cautioned, "Kurt, too many! No one wants to spend that much time watching unedited family videos."

Kurt was undaunted, putting the final tape in a bag. "We can sort through them later."

The next night we sat with Kevin and Manoela and Kyle and Katie in the living room of a rented condo. Kurt loaded the first tape into the VCR and there on the screen were two little boys playing football in the snow, Kyle's shoulder pads engulfing his five-year old frame, slapping against his body as he ran. Three-year old Kevin rushed after him, delighted to be part of the game. Laughter filled the frosty air.

My eyes watered. My voice shook. "Oh, Kurt… Wonderful times! Great memories!" After football we watched Kyle and Kevin playing hockey in the garage. Both boys chased a plastic baseball with hockey sticks meant for players twice their size. Kevin's giggles shook his entire body. Kyle smiled in big brotherly pride. More videos, more joy.

When Manoela had asked to see Kevin as a little boy, I had no idea how much I would enjoy seeing him too. Peals of laughter. Tears of joy. Giggles. I'd forgotten those times of childhood play when silliness filled a room, when one little boy raced after the other. They were "the days the Lord had made" and remembering King David's psalm, I rejoiced and was very glad.;e hand on Kevin's shoulder; the other's on Kyle's back. I'm smiling but squinting, my eyes betraying the emotion of a young mother.

In Chinese culture the azalea is known as the "thinking of home" bush. Now when I see an azalea, I think about home, our times together as a family, new times with extended family. These were—and are—the days the Lord has made and I rejoice and am glad.

> *Great Creator, you have made all of our days. Let us rejoice and be glad in every single one of them—the great ones full of giggles and even the ones that slid sideways. Amen.*

Digging Deeper

Describe your favorite family photo.

Have you had a chance to watch old video tapes or CDs and listen to the voices of your children? What was most memorable?

How do you rejoice in this day that the Lord has made, even when it's not one of your better days?

"You have Grandma's keys?"

14 Soothing Lemon Balm

"So do not fear, for I am with you; do not be dismayed, for I am your God. I will strengthen you and help you; I will uphold you with my righteous right hand."

- Isaiah 41:10 (NIV)

I winced, embarrassed, when my three-year old grandson Enzo walked up to a stranger on the sidewalk. "You have Grandma's keys?" A few minutes earlier he'd asked to go to the bathroom, so we'd taken a break from our lakeside stroll to return to his apartment building. But when I reached inside my pocket for the keys, nothing. Watching Enzo start to squirm, I quickly checked every pocket. No keys.

"Enzo, we need to go back to the dock. I think Grandma dropped her keys."

Ready to help, Enzo had turned to those nearby and begun asking, "You have Grandma's keys?" Fortunately, someone recognized Enzo and let us into his building—using their keys.

The next day I picked up my other grandson from daycare. Arriving at Austin's house, I unbuckled the straps of his car seat, set him on the ground, and closed the car door, not realizing he'd put his hand back into the opening. Unable to move, he screamed. I gripped the handle, threw open the car door, and gathered him into my arms, both of us sobbing. Fortunately, his little fingers were only pinched and not crunched.

For several weeks both boys reminded me of our difficult afternoons.

"Grandma, remember when you lost the keys and that lady helped us?"

Yes, Enzo.

"Grandma, remember when you pinched my fingers and we cried?"

Yes, Austin.

And then one afternoon, while sitting in his car seat, Enzo caught my eye in the rear-view mirror. Without mentioning the lost keys, he said, "Grandma, it happens."

The next day when I picked him up at daycare, Austin greeted me with a bouquet of lemon balm. "Smell my flowers, Grandma!"

"Oh, Austin, your momma will love them."

"They're for you, Grandma."

My carelessness met with their kindness. Assurance in the words, "It happens." A small bouquet. Love for a grandmother from two little boys. In my personal walk of faith, carelessness has also been met with kindness and assurance—when I've lost not only my keys but my direction, when I've hurt feelings as well as fingers. But God promises to be with us and forgive us.

"Fear not," writes the prophet Isaiah. "Do not be dismayed. God will keep you and strengthen you; he'll uphold you with his righteous right hand."

Enzo's words made me smile. The lemon scent from Austin's bouquet filled me with joy. Memories of their thoughtfulness soothe difficult memories. Also soothing were Austin's words after a visit to Disneyland. When asked by his dad about the best part of his day, he replied, "Holding Grandma's hand." Again, Grandma cried.

O Lord, we all have days of carelessness, yet you remain with us. We pray you would continue to strengthen us and help us. Uphold us in your righteousness. Amen.

Digging Deeper

Have you ever lost your keys? Done something careless that hurt someone else?

Who has given you "It happens" reassurance? Where were you? What happened?

Where can you share your own bouquet of lemon balm, figuratively or literally?

"Where is God? Is God even here?"

15 Hyssop and Mercy

"He saved us, not because of works done by us in righteousness, but according to his own mercy."

- Titus 3:5 (ESV)

Sitting in church at my neighbor's memorial service, I expected to see a cross. My own church has several. I stiffened. No cross. No altar either. I assumed a pastor would conduct the service, leading prayers and sharing a message, but the service was led by a family friend. No cross, no altar, no pastor, prayers, or sermon. I looked around. *Where is God?*

For an hour I fussed in my seat. How are we supposed to celebrate a life without celebrating the Creator of life? How can we know comfort and peace, hope and solace without remembering God's love and mercy? *Is God even here?*

At home later that day, I heard a knock. I opened the door and found my neighbor's friend with a bouquet of flowers from the service. In a vase were pink blooms of all shapes and sizes: feathery hyssop, delicate coral bells, spikes of salvia and foxglove, their collective scent heavenly. Looking at the flowers, I began to see how God had been in other details.

At the service I'd focused on all the things I thought missing, the things not done. But what I'd missed entirely were the ways in which God had been with us. He wasn't in the stuff; he was in us. I knew many people of faith had been at the service. I looked again at the bulletin we'd been given for the service. In it was a reference to prayer which had prompted me to share my own quiet prayer, several in fact. Yes, missing was a message, but I thought about the hope God would want us to feel and the love he would want us to share as we came together.

The bouquet from my neighbor's friend included hyssop. Hyssop was used to sprinkle the blood of sacrificial lambs on doorposts at Passover. A hyssop branch was also used to give Jesus a drink while he was dying on the cross, sacrificing his life for me and my neighbor, sharing his mercy with all of us. And in the pink belled flowers of the hyssop is the bigger message: What we do in a memorial service doesn't make us right with God; what God did on the cross makes us right with him.

The altar and the cross are important because they remind us of who God is and what he did. He saved us, not because we do the right thing at the right time or say the right words in the right place, but because of his mercy. I'd tried to make my neighbor's remembrance about doing and not doing, but it was really about honoring what God had done in the life of a very special lady.

> *O great God in heaven and on earth, we pause in humble gratitude for all you've done. You saved us, not because of anything we've done, but according to your mercy. Blessed be your name! Amen.*

What do you find most meaningful at a memorial service?

Have you ever found yourself not seeing God in a place where you expected to find him?

How has God been present in ways that surprised you?

"Why should I have to pay for your mistake?"

16

Forget-Me-Nots and Patience

"Better is the end of a thing than its beginning, and the patient in spirit is better than the proud in spirit."
- Ecclesiastes 7:8 (ESV)

I looked down at my needlework, five abstract hearts surrounded by "Live well, laugh often, love much." Pink swirls and purple stripes offset lime green lettering. Studying my stitching more closely, I paused, surprised. The colors were wrong. I'd been using a new skein of lime green yarn, but it didn't match the one I'd been using previously. ***Is it the same color but a different dye lot?*** I grabbed the tags. No, I'd been sent the wrong green, a closely-related green, but not the right green.

I called the needlepoint shop and explained the situation and was told there was nothing they could do. Because of the pandemic, they were unable to accept returns. I said I understood, but still I needed the correct green. I needed them to correct their mistake and send me the yarn I'd originally ordered. Days later the yarn arrived. To my dismay, a receipt was included for my payment of $11.63. Not pleased, I called the store.

"But you said you wanted the yarn."

"But *you* made the mistake. *You* sent the wrong green," I grumbled."Why should I have to pay for your mistake? Really! Would you risk losing a long-time customer over $11.63?"

Before I'd finished my question, I heard it: pettiness and impatience, the do-you-know-who-this-is tone in my voice. Would *I* risk losing a relationship with my favorite yarn shop over $11.63 during a pandemic misunderstanding?

During Covid, I tried to be a little more patient, a little more understanding. I over-tipped. I made bigger donations. And then what started as a minor inconvenience became a petulant grievance. So much for live, laugh, love. More like whine, complain, demand.

Words in Ecclesiastes may be more suitable for framing: "Better is the end of a thing than its beginning, and the patient in spirit is better than the proud in spirit." We can start with the best of intentions, the highest hopes, but irritations, big and small, can derail us. The end becomes worse than the beginning. Patience gives way to petulance or worse. I don't want bad endings in my life, and I certainly don't want pride to rule my day. I want to be kind. I also want to be patient.

One of the five hearts in my needlepoint is filled with pink forget-me-nots. In the garden, some forget-me-nots start with pink buds that open to blue blossoms, returning to a beautiful pink with age. I'd love to do the same—to start beautifully, age well, and end even more beautifully than I started. Oh, for a good beginning and a better ending.

Oh, for a patient heart while striving.

Dear God, help us remember the end of a thing is better than the beginning. May we overcome pride with patience, and may we all learn to live well, laugh often, and love much. Amen.

Did you have any impatient reactions during the pandemic? Endings that were not good?

Where has God shown you that the end of something was more important than the beginning?

How have you been able to live well, laugh often, and love much despite the circumstances?

"No more buts!"

Wonderfully Made Peonies

"I praise you, for I am fearfully and wonderfully made. Wonderful are your works; my soul knows it very well."
- Psalm 139:14 (ESV)

While walking the one-mile loop around a local lake, I looked ahead and smiled at a familiar face I'd not seen in over twenty years. Excited, I called out, "Hi! It's Deanna."

The other woman laughed and replied, "I remember you. I'm Diane."

For the next several minutes we reminisced and reconnected. Our boys had been in preschool together. They'd played on the same soccer team and graduated from high school the same year. Even though we'd not been sure about names, we easily remembered our shared past. She had taken my older son Kyle home from preschool. Her older daughter had made my lattes at a local drive-through.

Before saying goodbye and continuing our walks, Diane put her hand up in front of her shoulder-length gray hair, hiding the golden brown tips. She looked away as if embarrassed and went on to apologize for letting the color go. I was taken aback. Meeting her, I'd actually been struck by her beauty, the way her hair blew gently in the breeze, the peace and serenity in her eyes. How could she not see her beauty?

And then I remembered a card I'd gotten from Kurt. On the front were peonies and the words "To My Beautiful Wife..." Immediately I'd stopped. I could not get past the word beautiful. *But I've got another 10 pounds to lose... But I'm getting grayer by the day... But the wrinkles keep coming... But... But... But...* My wonderful husband of thirty-eight years had given me a lovely card, and I'd gotten stuck on a self-imposed *but*.

Too many of my days have started and ended with a critical assessment at the mirror. And that's after jumping on the scale with great hope and eager anticipation and then stepping off with a heavy sigh. Too often my internal dialog is unkind and unloving. *But you're still overweight. But you look old.* In my own way, I put up my hand and try to hide, adding another *but* to my day.

When King David exclaims we are fearfully and wonderfully made, I have difficulty including myself in such praise. Mired in *but* after *but*, I struggle to treasure God's creativity. I grouse about failing eyesight, tired joints, and that next ten pounds to lose. I'm focused on what I perceive as design flaws.

We are surrounded by powerful images and messages. Some encourage us to be all we can be; some promote who and what we should be. When I ran into Diane, I began to appreciate the impact of the *buts* in my life, and the next morning, standing in front of the mirror, I said aloud, "No more *buts*!" Instead I tried to see myself as David saw himself: fearfully and wonderfully made by God.

Lush peony blossoms decorated the front of Kurt's card. Pink petals with darker pink tips, blooms of different sizes and shapes. Mixed in were buds not yet open, each one wonderfully made in its own way, each one worthy of praise. As we all are.

To our Heavenly Creator, we praise you for we are fearfully and wonderfully made! Your works are wonderful, and we are blessed to be a beautiful part of it. Amen.

Digging Deeper

When you think about yourself, where have you used the word "but"?

Write out the words to Psalm 139:14. Now read the verse out loud.

> *"I praise you, for I am fearfully and wonderfully made. Wonderful are your works; my soul knows it very well."*

Describe how you're fearfully and wonderfully made.

"Oh, God! Please, God!"

18 Clematis and Cords of Strength

"A cord of three strands is not quickly broken."
- Ecclesiastes 4:12 (NIV)

During the Covid outbreak, our "new normal" unsettled me. I had on-line conference calls that went poorly. I had regrettable conversations with my contact person at the corporate office. I had a petty, self-indulgent rant when nail salons closed. I even had a "panic buying" moment that resulted in a case of commercial-grade toilet paper that was thinner than tissue paper with the consistency of waxed paper. And then one night, I forgot the words to the Lord's Prayer.

I've been saying the Lord's Prayer since I was a small child sitting in a church pew, my skinny little legs too short to reach the floor. The words have been part of my prayer life for decades. I even have the words crocheted and framed on my office wall. Yep, that prayer!

While social distancing, our church leadership team met virtually Monday nights. We closed with the Lord's Prayer. Everyone muted the microphone on their computer and let me lead. One night, after three sentences, I forgot the words. Nothing. *Oh, God! Please, God!* Nothing. Finally, after an uncomfortably long silence, Pastor Todd unmuted himself and finished the prayer.

It was a humbling moment. I'm used to reciting the prayer with others and without others around me, I faltered. I'm also used to doing life with others around me. While social distancing, I faltered many times, not just in words to a prayer but in response to life's new ups and downs.

Too often I got self-absorbed and small-minded, whiny and intolerant. My unraveling also impacted my relationship with God. Not only did I physically separate from those around me, but I began to distance myself from God too. My prayers got smaller. My Bible study got shorter and then stopped altogether. My heart cooled. My anxiety heated up.

In the Old Testament book of Ecclesiastes, Solomon talks about how a cord of three strands twisted together isn't quickly broken. One person can be overpowered, two can resist, but strength is found in a third person. During the pandemic, I was a single strand with fraying ends, sniveling about a missed manicure and hoarding paper products. Then one cold, dark winter morning I met friends for coffee, masked up and bundled up outside our favorite gathering place. These four very special ladies became my second cord of resistance with their encouragement, comfort, and gentle refocus from petty complaints. Strength came in the third cord: God. I confessed my ridiculous attitude and asked God's forgiveness. A cord of three strands twisted together: me, my friends, and God.

A Clematis jackmanii climbs a trellis in my front yard. Left unattended, the plant will creep along in search of something—anything—on which to twist and climb, the flowers inevitably getting lost in a tangle of nearby azalea branches. To be its most beautiful, the clematis needs water and sunshine—and the support of the trellis. We're no different. We all need help in our "new normal." And with God and each other we have the strength needed. We won't be easily broken.

Dearest Lord Jesus, we are blessed to be part of a cord that includes you and your people. May we always find our strength in you. Amen.

Describe a time when you felt isolated. What surprised you about the situation?

How has a three-stranded cord with God and others strengthened you during challenges?

Where can you be part of a three-stranded cord for someone?

"You wanna race?"

19 Rhododendrons and Love

"...walk in love which is the bond of perfection."
- Colossians 3:14 (WEB)

I met my buddy when he was thirteen and living across the street with his grandma and step-grandpa. One day while riding my bike I waved at him. The next day I waved and said, "Hi!" The third day he was waiting for me on his own bicycle, an amused twinkle in his eye. "You wanna race?"

I smiled and said, "Sure!" not really sure I should be racing a seventh grader at my age.

In addition to racing, my buddy and I started having small conversations about school and those never-ending homework assignments. Not knowing his grandparents and not wanting to cross any safety boundaries, I never asked his name. I just thought of him as "my buddy." I waved whenever I saw him, smiled and giggled whenever he wanted to race, groaned when he described multiplication problems with two and three digits. I never imagined we would find ourselves together in the rain under an overgrown rhododendron the day medics arrived to help his grandma.

I watched the first of nine emergency vehicles rush into our neighborhood on a cold, wet, miserable Friday morning and stop at the brick house across the street—my buddy's house. First an aid car, then a firetruck and police cruiser. Lights flashed. First responders ran into the yard. I hurried outside, wondering what had happened, unsure how to help. And then I saw him. In the middle of the chaos was my buddy, standing alone, medics rushing past him.

I crossed the street. "Hey, what's going on?"

"Grandma's not doing well. She's been getting weaker and weaker. Today we had to call 911."

Soon an emergency medical technician came out of the house and told us Grandma was doing terribly and needed a lot of help. After twenty-five minutes, another EMT let us know they were continuing CPR. He asked my buddy not to give up hope. Twenty-five minutes later he rushed to where we were standing. "We found a pulse! It's weak, but we've still got hope. That means you've gotta have hope."

Standing next to my buddy, I offered to pray for Grandma's well-being. He took my hand and I began. I was not at my finest. I rambled. I repeated myself. I stumbled trying to find the right words, but in the confusion and chaos, our hearts heavy with concern, I was able to thank God for being with us, for providing Grandma with the finest care, for giving my buddy and the EMTs hope. Most important, I was able to remind my buddy of God's love for each one of us.

In Colossians, Paul asks us to "walk in love which is the bond of perfection." Love is a glue that can hold neighbors together, especially when times are hard. I "walked in love" racing bikes with my buddy. I also "walked in love" standing with him under a large wet rhododendron, the day I learned his real name was Bryson, but everyone calls him Buddy.

Dearest Lord, help us find ways to walk in love with our neighbor and be the glue that holds us together with those around us. Amen.

Digging Deeper

When have you been able to "walk in love" with a neighbor? Did any of those small moments lead to bigger ones?

Remembering Colossians 3:14, what does a "walk in love" look like in your life?

Any neighbors who need you to "walk in love" with them?

"Maybe, just maybe, I don't know it all."

Calla Lilies and Arrogance

"Seek his will in all you do, and he will show you which path to take."

- Proverbs 3:6 (NLT)

Too often I think I know everything. I'll question authority, push the limits, defy the rules, always insisting I have the last word. I actually drove around the block eight times one night in high school just to make sure I got home late. My know-it-all attitude has colored my relationship with my parents, my teachers, even God who I assumed was just another imposing authority figure dictating what I should do and how I should do it.

When my husband and I moved to Monroe, Washington, a local pastor stopped by the house and extended an invitation to "Give us a try." The neighborhood church was only a couple blocks away. I was intrigued. Perhaps an hour on Sunday, a couple hymns, and a good sermon would be a nice addition to life with my husband and young sons. Should any childrearing episodes result in a parenting disaster, I'd be able to confess my shortcomings and leave with a little forgiveness and a chance at a fresh start on Monday.

So, the family and I went to church. In addition to worshiping each Sunday, I was soon planning church celebrations, playing my violin, leading meetings, and sharing prayers, still not taking any advice or counsel from God or anyone else, still thinking I knew everything about everything. My arrogance came into sharp focus when I decided how best to "help" with our Wednesday night program for elementary school kids.

I was somewhat familiar with the midweek program, but I didn't know its goals or its objectives. I did know the children were louder than I thought appropriate in a church building. But rather than speak with the leader or the parents and volunteers involved, I barged in with all the changes I thought best.

And our Wednesday nights were awful. My insistence on order had the kids almost marching between dinner and outdoor play, Bible lessons and music time. The only thing missing was Captain von Trapp's whistle. My constant "Inside voices!" left the children unsure how to enjoy themselves. Before I could smile and loosen up a bit, they were pleading with their parent to go home and not come back.

Steve, the leader, took me aside after the third week. "Deanna," he said, "we appreciate your willingness to help on Wednesdays." Using his "inside voice," he suggested, "Perhaps a little less regimentation and a little more fun?"

In one of the Proverbs is an admonition to seek God's will in all we do, not something I was doing Wednesday nights. Or other nights! Solomon knew God would show us the path to take. I began to see that path in my conversation with Steve.

Before going home that night, I went and sat in the church which was dark and empty, but light enough for me to see calla lilies on the altar. I smiled at the beauty of the tall bell-shaped blooms. They always remind me of God, whether blooming in my garden or rising tall in church. In the quiet of the moment, I said aloud, "Maybe, just maybe, I don't know it all." Rolling my eyes at my struggles, praying God might appreciate my humor, I added, "Maybe, just maybe, you do."

Dearest Lord, help us seek your will in all we do. Show us the path to take. Amen.

Any know-it-all moments times when you were younger? As an adult?

When have you needed help to see God's will for you?

Who has been there to show you God's path for your life?

"Oh! My! Goodness!"

21 Bishop's Weed and Grace

"For by grace you have been saved through faith. And this is not your own doing; it is the gift of God."

- Ephesians 2:8 (ESV)

I set my phone on the roof of the car and buckled Austin into his car seat, our playdate over and time to take him home. After heading down the road, I turned onto a four-lane highway. Picking up speed, I heard a loud clunk-clunk. ***What was that? Did I run over something? Did a rock just hit my car?*** And then it really hit me: my phone!

"Austin, did you hear that funny noise? Grandma left her phone on top of the car and I think it just fell off. I need to turn around and see if I can find it."

"But where, Grandma?"

That was the question: But where?

After parking on a small siding road, I got out of the car and looked out over the highway. I kicked at the knee-high grass along the edge. I peered into an abundance of Bishop's Weed and scowled. ***Are these delicate, pretty flowers hiding my phone?*** I gave another kick at the lacy white profusion of ground cover before I walked to the front of my car. I took another look out over the highway before I walked behind my car. And then, turning around, I saw it. Stuck in the frame of the rear window was my phone. It must have bounced off the roof and slipped down the glass before getting lodged in the lower edge of the frame.

"Oh! My! Goodness!" Looking up, I said out loud, "God, there is nothing I've done today to deserve this. Nothing. Not a single thing."

Nothing yesterday either.

I expected to find my phone in pieces in the center lane of a major highway, smashed by a large truck racing to beat a nearby traffic light while driving into town. If not smashed, at least cracked and scratched. But no, I found my phone in one piece, not a scratch on it.

While walking the next day, I caught sight of another clump of Bishop's Weed and thought back to my roadside drama. I'd been overwhelmed by my stroke of luck, my ***undeserved*** good fortune. I began thinking about God's grace and my ***undeserved*** forgiveness. Grace manifested by forgiveness is a tenet of my faith, but it's rare I get to glimpse its enormity. More often I'm focused on what I "deserve" in life. ***I'm a good person, so... I work hard, so...*** I choose to ignore the times I'm rummaging through "weeds," letting thoughtlessness and carelessness rule the day, the times I deserve the consequences of my actions.

But God forgives our carelessness, our thoughtlessness, our sins. We are saved by his grace wherever we might be, no matter the circumstances. The apostle Paul writes that this is not of our own doing. A lucky break? No, an undeserved gift of God.

God doesn't always intercede in our lost-phone adventures. But sometimes I wonder if he doesn't use our carelessness and good fortune as a godsend, helping us better see and more deeply appreciate the "Oh! My! Goodness!" gifts in our relationship with him.

My Lord and Savior, we thank you for your undeserved grace. Help us better see and appreciate the hugeness of this wonderful gift. Amen.

Digging Deeper

When have you gotten a "lucky break"?

Any experiences that were an "Oh! My! Goodness!" lesson in God's grace?

Is there a way to more deeply appreciate God's grace without a "lost phone" episode?

"My mom has one just like it."

22 Forced Paperwhites

"And Mary said, 'Behold, I am the servant of the LORD; let it be to me according to your word...'"

- Luke 1:38 (ESV)

One Christmas before we married, Kurt stopped by my parents' house, carrying a large gift. "Here!" he said, handing me the package, merry and bright.

Sitting down together, I hesitated. I'd expected Kurt to show up with a much smaller box. Unwrapping his present, I looked inside at a frying pan. ***A frying pan! Really? A frying pan?***

Kurt smiled. "My mom has one just like it. She uses it for everything."

A frying pan!?!

"Talk to Mom. She fries chicken in hers. She even makes toasted cheese sandwiches and scrambled eggs."

I needed no cooking suggestions from Kurt. After five years of dating, I was not thinking about life's culinary possibilities. I wanted marriage. I wanted to connect with Kurt in a more meaningful way and not while cooking together in the kitchen. I wanted a small box with a ring inside. I ached for a sparkler that would light up the future, something that twinkled ***I'm loved!*** I longed for a 14-karat beacon of joy to the world that announced ***I'm getting married!***

When the angel Gabriel appeared to Mary, she and Joseph were already engaged. They'd already announced to their family and friends they were getting married. But then an angel brought news Mary was going to have a baby, God's own Son. The shock had to have been staggering. *God's son! Really? God's Son?*

What would Mary have been thinking and feeling hearing the angel's announcement? Did she hesitate? Did she catch her breath before accepting God's will for her life? Before she replied, "May it be to me as you have said"?

I did not look at the frying pan and think, *May it be to me as you would want, Lord.* I pouted. I didn't want to heat up chicken in a frying pan; I wanted to heat up my relationship with Kurt. I didn't want to stir together scrambled eggs; I wanted to stir together wedding plans.

Some of us have a tradition of forcing paperwhites to bloom at Christmas. Bulbs are placed in a shallow bowl on top of rocks. With water and sunshine, they put down roots and bloom in four to six weeks, bright spots of spring color in the middle of winter's darkness.

Early in our relationship, my heart was set on life with Kurt and, because of that, I wanted to force decisions. Too often I had our relationship sitting on top of rocks. I knew bigger decisions in life shouldn't be forced, not at Christmas or any other time. Still, I wanted what I wanted.

Paperwhites are also known as narcissus. Sounds like narcissism, doesn't it? Which sounds a lot like self-centeredness. My reaction to Kurt's Christmas gift was a self-centered response, not a "May it be to me as you have said" respect for God's plans. That lesson would take another four years for me to accept while I learned to appreciate God's will and his timing.

> *Father in heaven, as life unfolds, help us learn to appreciate your will, your way, and your when. Help us find the words, "May it be to me as you have said." Amen.*

Have you ever gotten a Christmas gift that surprised you? Perhaps disappointed you?

Has there been a time when you've needed to say, "God, may it be to me as you have said"?

How have God's plans and his timing been perfect in your life?

"Why do you insist on using my fuchsia basket?

Fuchsias and Endurance

"...endurance produces character..."
- Romans 5:4 (ESV)

The bird's shrieks were loud and insistent. ***It's happened again!*** In a nearby tree, I spotted the mother who was trying to divert my attention with high-pitched chirps. I turned and walked across the lawn to my front door and carefully unhooked a basket of fuchsias from the trellis. Intricately woven into the plant was a nest of twigs and leaves, bits of paper and yarn. Four bluish gray eggs lay in the middle. *Yes, it had happened again. Three years in a row!*

I looked out at the mother bird. "Why do you insist on using my fuchsia basket for a nest when you *know* I'm out here watering every few days?!" Twice a week I'd been flooding the basket, even adding plant fertilizer on occasion. How had the eggs survived?

A week later Momma became less patient and more aggressive. No longer just chirping, she was now flying straight for me, narrowly missing my head at times. Her babies must have hatched! Curious, I again unhooked the basket. This time I found four downy-feathered hatchlings in the nest, their eyes closed and their mouths open in anticipation of lunch.

"Oh, Momma, your babies are wonderful!"

For three years, this mother bird had chosen my fuchsia basket for her nest. For three years, I'd watered the basket every three days for a month before finding her eggs. I looked around at all the neighboring trees and larger shrubs, wondering why my fuchsias. She had to have known I'd be watering, that the possibility of flooding was very real, yet she'd endured challenge after challenge.

We've all found ourselves facing challenges and times when we've needed to endure trials in our life. I'd decided to become an elementary school teacher in college; my parents were teachers. But after settling into my own classroom, I realized teaching was not the place for me. I was devastated and distraught, flooded with doubts. *Do I belong in education? Am I supposed to be a teacher?*

I didn't. I wasn't. And while I figured out where I would go next, I had responsibilities to meet. Eighteen children needed me at my finest. They needed lessons prepared, math assignments checked, and spelling tests given. I had to honor them, despite my career uncertainties.

Paul wrote in Romans that endurance produces character. But when facing challenges, we're not thinking about endurance. When I realized I needed to leave teaching, I wanted out of the classroom right then. I certainly didn't want to become a character study in patience and determination, but I had a contract to fulfill. It would be a year before I could say goodbye, twelve months of character development.

The momma bird in my fuchsia basket endured big challenges. I had to endure too. Working through my career difficulties, I had to stick it out for longer than I would have liked, but in the process, I developed a stronger sense of self. I learned the real value of commitments made, of responsibilities needing attention. And in time, I learned to appreciate the complexities of transition.

This year the momma bird did not come back to my fuchsia basket. I wonder if she found a better place to nest like I did.

Dearest Lord, help us endure, knowing endurance produces character. Amen.

Any nests found where you didn't expect them?

Describe a time when you've had to endure a difficult situation.

How has endurance produced character in your own life?

"Goodnight, Thorp."

24 Violets and Peace

"Peace I leave with you; my peace I give to you. Not as the world gives do I give to you. Let not your hearts be troubled, neither let them be afraid."

- John 14:27 (ESV)

Kurt decided we should clean out the attic. I was intrigued, opening boxes not touched in decades. We found my first resume—height and weight included—along with an '80's hot-roller hair photo. We found canceled checks from my first year of teaching. We discovered my autograph book from 5th grade and a set of delicate teacups trimmed with lavender violets, a gift from Grandma.

But painful memories also surfaced. After finding three carousel trays of old 35mm slides, Kurt set up the old screen, plugged in the old projector, and clicked through dozens of dusty slides from college and our early years together. Pictures with friends at the beach, at a campsite, in the neighborhood where we lived after getting married, family gatherings with cousins. Many images were as blurry as the memories themselves. But one of the last slides was in sharp focus: a picture of me, my head to the side glancing back at the camera. I'm young and sickly thin, my protruding breast bones clearly visible in the afternoon sun, my waif-like arms hiding nothing. I was stunned. Memories of my eating disorder flooded over me.

"Kurt, it's hard remembering that time in my life. I was so miserable. I couldn't cope, couldn't care for myself, couldn't accept myself."

"Focus on the journey. That's where you *were*. It's not where you are *now*. Think about how far you've come."

How far I've come. But the journey continues. The girl who lived in so much pain is still a part of me. The teenager plagued by perceived imperfections still questions her adult abilities. The young woman flailing in her attempts to figure it out still flails as a grownup.

And aren't we all just trying to figure it out—whatever "it" might be? Attic boxes were reminiscent of my journey so far, struggles and challenges as well as opportunities and accomplishments. Mementos were sorted into "Keep" and "Don't Keep" piles, a process I found surprising peaceful as I came to terms with my now-and-then and up-and-down journey. I tossed the old slides, but kept Grandma's teacups, setting them beside lavender violets on my window sill.

The apostle Paul speaks of "peace of God that surpasses all understanding" (Philippians 4:7). I think this is the peace I began to experience while sorting through old stuff from the attic, when I began to see and appreciate who I was and who I've become. It's the peace Jesus spoke of when he said he would leave us with his peace. *Don't be worried and upset,* he tells us gently. *Don't be afraid.* I think he would want me to not only focus on the journey, but to be at peace with it.

Kurt often calls me Thorp, my maiden name. My day ends with "Goodnight, Thorp," simple words that honor the young woman I was. The woman I am today smiles. And the woman I will become is at peace about tomorrow.

Dearest Lord Jesus, we thank you for being with us in our journey. Help us find your peace, the peace that surpasses all understanding. Amen.

Any memorable finds in the attic? Your garage?

Is there an old, dusty box that still weighs heavily on you?

Where has God shown you peace in your own journey?

"Grandma, you found me!"

25 Ornamental Grass and Reassurance

"The LORD himself goes before you and will be with you; he will never leave you nor forsake you. Do not be afraid; do not be discouraged."

- Deuteronomy 31:8 (NIV)

"Grandma, you found me!"

Enzo was at a new summer camp. I smiled at him swimming in the pool. "Enzo, Grandma will always find you."

Helping Enzo out of the water, I remembered a time when I was six years old and said the same thing, "Dad, you found me!" Mom and I were supposed to take the train home after a visit to Grandma's house, but it derailed and we had to take the bus. The hushed conversations and hurried arrangements made me anxious. The change in plans frightened me. Boarding the bus, Mom handed me a coloring book and crayons, but I was too distracted for artwork.

Handing Enzo a towel, I told him my story. "Even though I was sitting with my mom, I felt lost. My dad was planning to pick us up at the train station. I didn't know how he would find me at the bus station. I was afraid and worried the whole way."

"The whole way, Grandma?"

"Yes, the whole way."

"But when the bus pulled into the station in Seattle, I looked out my window and saw Dad! He'd found me! My mom had called him and told him where I'd be. And you know what, Enzo? Your dad called me today and told me where you'd be!"

I wonder if our prayers are a similar call to our heavenly Father when plans change and we feel lost, when we might fear where we're going and worry about how to get there. In Deuteronomy, Moses writes that God goes before us and is with us; he will never leave us or forsake us. We don't need to be afraid. God knows where we'll be when life derails, whether we're at the bus station or summer camp, wherever change takes us.

In first grade, after my visit to Grandma, I colored a picture of the train I'd expected to take home. The engine is purple with a red caboose and blue passenger car. In a big blue sky is a small black cloud. In front of the engine are broken tracks. Just ahead, a brown overhang, perhaps the roof of the train station or maybe the bus station. In the grass are tall green clumps. No flowers, just long green stems, a six-year old's version of ornamental grass. The picture's bold colors and detailed images capture my fear and anxiety as well as my relief at being found.

When the train derailed, I'd been worried and afraid, but Dad had known where I was and where I'd be. The memory helps me better understand how God can know where I am and where I'll be; where we all are, where we all will be. I hope Enzo will remember being found and feel that same reassurance.

Dearest God, thank you for going before us and promising to be with us. Help us not to worry. Amen.

Digging Deeper

Did you ever get lost as a child? What happened? Who found you?

As an adult, have you ever felt lost? In a job or relationship? At a certain age or during a particular season?

When has God been at "the bus station" when life derailed and new plans had to be made?

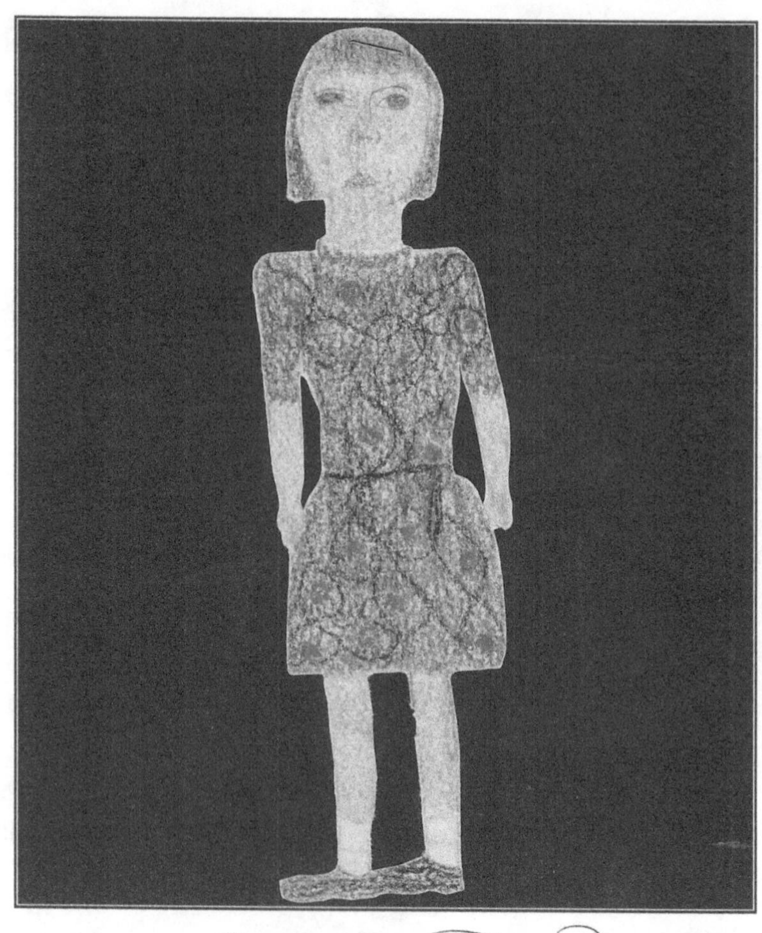

"What a joy to be with you!"

26 Chrysanthemums and Gratitude

"Therefore, as you received Christ Jesus the LORD, so walk in him, rooted and built up in him and established in the faith, just as you were taught, abounding in thanksgiving."
- Colossians 2:6-7 (ESV)

Standing at the podium, I looked out at the group of twenty-eight older women and smiled.

"Hello! What a joy to be with you."

I was back at Trinity Lutheran Church, the speaker for "An Evening with a Daughter", and I was the daughter. I'd grown up at Trinity, been baptized in the old church, married in the new. We were meeting in the Fireside Room, a cozy, wood-paneled gathering place that looked out over the courtyard where I'd played Red Rover during Vacation Bible School. We were next door to the classroom where I'd taught Sunday School. In the adjoining kitchen, I'd volunteered at wedding receptions. My first "real" job had been in the church office after school and on weekends.

I was delighted to reconnect after almost twenty years. In my speech, I talked about how our ordinary lives connect to God's extraordinary love and faithfulness and how their love and care had connected me to God's love and care. As the daughter of the church, I knew I was talking to a group of moms who had not only raised their own children—my friends—but also me. I'd spent mornings before school with Alice and afternoons at church with Connie. My brother and I went to school with Carole's children. Susie's girls too. Carol's brother-in-law was my sixth-grade teacher. Anita lived around the corner from my family and taught at Parkland School with Mom.

These women had supported and encouraged me when I was a child and young teen. They'd impacted me in ways I hadn't thought about before then. Not only had Alice provided breakfast before school when Mom began substitute teaching, she'd had a ready smile and wonderful words of encouragement. Connie had given me a job and responsibilities when I'd been a struggling teen, a position at church remarkably similar to my eventual position in finance. Carol and Susie, together with my own mom, coordinated VBS each summer, organized Christmas programs, and started mid-week youth gatherings. When we got back together, I knew I'd be sharing giggles about those itchy halos from the Christmas program, but that I'd also get to share memories of care and encouragement, love and guidance.

Paul reminds the Colossians to walk with Jesus, being rooted in faith, abounding in thanksgiving. I'd been rooted in my faith at Trinity with the help of these women, and my return abounded in thanksgiving.

I came home from my visit with a "Thank You!" pot of bright yellow chrysanthemums. I planted them in my front garden as a reminder of the moms who had rooted me in my faith. And each year when they bloom, I remember and abound in thanksgiving.

God, our father in heaven, keep us rooted and built up in our faith. Let us abound in thanksgiving. Amen

Digging Deeper

Growing up, who helped nurture your faith?

Have you ever had a chance to thank them? If yes, when? If not, is there a way to do so now?

Who might you mentor in their faith?

I expected to be overjoyed…

Solomon's Seal and Discernment

"It pleased the LORD that Solomon asked this."
- 1 Kings 3:10 (ESV)

A clump of Solomon's Seal flourishes in the back corner of my garden, flowers that have become a perennial favorite. The plant's arching stems are about eighteen inches high. At the tip, small creamy blossoms hang in a six-inch curve of white. I don't know how the plant found its shady place in my yard, but it continues to surprise and delight me every spring. Its name and unusual appearance make me think about King Solomon and his request for discernment.

Solomon is said to have been the wisest of Israel's kings, wise enough to start his reign by asking for what was important: a discerning heart to govern God's people and the knowledge of right and wrong (1 Kings 3:9).

I haven't always known what's most important, especially when it comes to my weight. We all have our issues, but for me, weight and weight loss have consumed me since I was fifteen. Every morning I have used the scale to determine my self-worth, my self-confidence, my self-esteem. My weight has dictated the direction of my day. A pound up and I'm disappointed, discouraged, disheartened. A pound down and I'm smiling, ready for anything.

Recently I stood on the bathroom scale, once again watching the digital numbers flash. I was down ninety pounds from an awful high point! I was finally at a weight that had eluded me for twenty-five years. I stepped into the shower, grabbed the shampoo, and smiled. Later in the day I had a playdate with Austin. A beautiful fall day was in the forecast. We'd be able to hang out in his backyard. We might even find the "monster" who lurked in nearby bushes.

While rinsing my hair, I thought about an upcoming trip with Kurt to Palm Springs, our favorite destination for rest and relaxation. Time together in the desert always included long walks and longer talks, special coffee and movie dates.

Getting dressed, I looked in the mirror. For years, my #1 focus had been dieting, calories in, calories out, low fat, low carbs, no sugar. And now after losing so much weight, I expected to feel ecstatic. I was certainly happy, but I expected to be overjoyed, over the moon, and I wasn't.

Because weight no longer consumed my thoughts and defined my day. After years of struggle, I'd slowly been able to let go of an unhealthy obsession with food to focus on self-care one bite at a time. And while learning to make healthy choices, I'd been able to more fully enjoy my life, turning my focus from the scale to afternoon giggles and a trip with my husband. Perhaps that's why I'd been so underwhelmed: Something more important had tipped the scale.

Solomon asked for discernment that he might govern his people well. I needed discernment, so I could better govern my own life. The next ten pounds and tomorrow's dress size are not what's most important; the people I love and my time with them are.

Lord of all, help us "govern" our lives well. May our choices reflect discernment and what's most important. Amen.

Digging Deeper

Have you found any unexpected blooms in your garden?

Any long-term challenges in your life?

Where in your life have you needed discernment? What "tipped the scale" for you?

"Really, I'm fine! I'm just late for my appointment."

28

Scotch Broom, Hasty Words, and Noxious Thoughts

"Let the words of my mouth and the meditation of my heart be acceptable in your sight, O LORD, my rock and my redeemer."

- Psalm 19:14 (ESV)

When I'm frantic, I resort to pitiful "Please, God! Please, God!" prayers, and one Wednesday God had to hear my plaintive whining over and over again. I had an appointment for an MRI as part of a high-risk breast cancer study. My mother, her sister, and a cousin have all had breast cancer and even though I don't have the known cancer genes, I've been asked to continue twice yearly screenings, not only for my own health, but also to help figure out why some of us develop breast cancer and some of us don't.

Living in the Seattle area, I give myself plenty of time to navigate traffic—except that day I didn't. At the freeway, I joined a two-mile backup, the overhead digital display alerting me to an accident three exits ahead. I had no time for a delay. Crawling ever so slowly, I repeated, "Please, God! Please, God!" When I finally passed the accident, the snarl now behind me, I raced ahead, taking advantage of every open gap between cars. I darted from lane to lane, determined to make up time.

I entered the hospital at 3:30 for my 2:45 appointment and was immediately stopped by a health screener. Looking at my watch, my frustration becoming seismic, I snapped, "Ma'am, I'm healthy! But I'm late for an appointment! Very late! I need you to use that phone beside you to call Radiology and let them know I'm here. And then I need you to clear me for entry STAT."

She did not call Radiology. Ignoring my rudeness, she handed me a list of Covid symptoms and asked about any recent exposure. "No! No! I'm fine! Really, I'm fine! I'm just late for my appointment."

Ignoring my exasperation, adhering to her check-in procedures, she took my temperature, confirmed my vaccination status, and finally—finally!—cleared me for entry. I dashed into the imaging department and was greeted by a young woman who suggested I catch my breath. They were forty-five minutes behind and would be ready for me shortly.

Forty-five minutes behind! I was incensed. *Really! You mean if I'd been on time for my appointment, I would have been waiting forty-five minutes!*

I turned sharply and headed to the waiting room. *Forty-five minutes behind!* And then it happened: My shoulders slumped, my heart softened, my anger began to ease. *Oh, God!* I grimaced. *Here I am forty-five minutes late for an appointment where they're forty-five minutes behind schedule and my first reaction is indignation. Please forgive me.*

Leaving the hospital, I apologized to the screener. She assured me traffic can strain us all. "Yes," I said, "but that didn't give me the right to speak to you as I did."

Mustard-colored scotch broom lines the freeway to and from the hospital. It's a noxious weed that spreads aggressively, displacing native plants and grasslands. Attitudes and actions can also do this, I shamefully realized. Long ago King David wrote, "Let my words be acceptable to you, O God." Mine too.

O Lord, let our words and thoughts be acceptable to you.
You are our rock and redeemer. Amen.

When has traffic been an issue for you?

Any go-to prayers for times of stress?

How can you keep your words and thoughts acceptable to God?

"I need your attention. Now!"

Baby's Breath and Tone of Voice

"Let your speech always be gracious, seasoned with salt, so that you may know how you ought to answer each person."

- Colossians 4:6 (ESV)

Kurt and I enjoy a week with our sons, Kyle and Kevin, and their families every summer at a resort on the Columbia River in Washington State. We swim in the pool, waterski on the river, and swing at the playground. Last summer I helped our four-year-old grandsons get ready for the three-hour drive home. I gave them a snack of crackers and cheese and a few grapes and said, "Enzo and Austin, I need you to go to the bathroom. Then we'll grab our backpacks and head to the car."

Enzo immediately went; Austin did not.

Using my stern seventh-grade teacher voice, I launched into a louder than necessary call to action. "Guys, I need your attention. Now. We are all going to go to the bathroom. Now. All of us. *Now!*"

Enzo reminded me he'd just gone; Austin started to cry, alarmed by the tone of my voice. And now he was so upset he couldn't have gone to the bathroom even if he'd wanted to.

Reflecting back, I can rationalize the importance of my request. I can justify how we all needed to do our part, how the ride home was going to be long, bathrooms not always available. But I spoke to two little boys like they were misbehaving seventh graders, not preschoolers needing a little help and guidance.

The apostle Paul tells the Colossians that our speech should be gracious, in order to answer each person as we should. I did not speak to Enzo and Austin as I should. I was not gracious. I wasn't just firm; I was overbearing. I didn't just organize our departure; I gave two four-year-olds their marching orders.

After we got in the car, we were minutes into our drive when I realized I'd forgotten to use the bathroom myself. Yep. Ironically, the four-year old who didn't need to go outlasted his cousin—who *had* gone. And his grandmother—who *hadn't*.

A bouquet of flowers had been sitting on the counter of our rented condo, a beautiful backdrop to a not-so-beautiful moment with my grandsons. Miniature sunflowers, powdery blue hydrangeas, deep purple lisianthus, and whitish green snapdragons came together in a profusion of color. Throughout the mix were sprigs of baby's breath, filling the gaps gracefully and delicately, adding a light, airy feel to the arrangement. My *"Now!"* had not filled our preparations gracefully and delicately. Nor had it created a "Let's go! We can do this!" tone of excitement for our departure. Instead, my words ended our week with tears and anxiety.

After we got home, I apologized to the boys, "Enzo and Austin, Grandma didn't speak very nicely when we were getting ready to leave. I'm very sorry." I spoke with them graciously, not as misbehaving seventh-graders but as four-year-olds. As I should have done in the beginning. Enzo again reminded me he'd gone when first asked.

And Austin smiled and gave me a hug.

Father in heaven, let our speech be gracious, so that we may answer each person in the way we should. Amen.

Digging Deeper

Describe a time when the tone of your voice changed the direction of a conversation—and not in a good way.

Can you think of a time when the tone of your voice was more important than the words said?

How do gracious words help us answer each person as we should?

"That I can promise you."

Camellias and God's Care

"casting all your anxieties on him, because he cares for you."

- 1 Peter 5:7 (ESV)

I met my mother-in-law Phyllis after a football game during my sophomore year at Pacific Lutheran University. She was there to support her son, the starting right guard; I was there to cheer on my favorite guy. That crisp fall day may have been about football, but I would learn her life was about faith, family, and an unwavering trust in God's care.

Phyllis loved time with family, whether watching her son play football or celebrating the holidays. She delighted in her grandchildren picking blueberries from her backyard bushes. She treasured holidays playing card games after dinner. She enjoyed sharing homemade applesauce with loved ones. In later years, her great-grandchildren Enzo and Austin picked berries from the same bushes and found the same card games in a storage closet. They also loved her applesauce.

In her last months, Phyllis and I had more and more time together as she prepared to move to an assisted living facility, a big change. Assuming she might be anxious, I spent many afternoons talking about what would happen next, when changes would be made, how this next phase in life would look. While I was trying to help her look ahead, she became more and more reflective. She remembered walking home from church on Sunday, December 7, 1941 when she learned about the bombing of Pearl Harbor from neighbors in the street. She was ten. She talked about the family's unexpected move when her husband George became a high school principal. She described the heartbreak of a loved one's suicide and the loneliness she experienced after her husband's death.

Our chats gave me a bigger glimpse into the faith that underscored her life. I saw it in her appreciation for the love and support of family; I heard it in her reflections. No words of frustrations accompanied unexpected twists. No feelings of regret for unforeseen turns. No "if only" sighs. No unkindness or unforgiveness. Just warm, tender memories of God's care for her and her family.

Phyllis and I often chatted at the kitchen table while watching the birds outside her window. Chickadees and sparrows darted in and out of an old, fifteen-foot, misshapen camellia bush. The shrub had missing limbs and lower branches. At times I wondered if the overgrown, lopsided, gangly thing needed to be removed, but Phyllis wouldn't hear of it. Not only was it home to her feathered friends, but it lit up her garden with eye-catching, late winter blooms, deep pink with gold centers.

One afternoon while looking at a camellia blossom floating in a dish on the table, I smiled with renewed appreciation for the depth of her faith, her love of family, and her trust in God's care. I thought about her and the beauty that comes from a life well lived, misshapen though it may be, the color that awaits us all at the end of winter, the abundance of blessings yet to come. I thought my visits had been reassurance for Phyllis, but our chats and her reflections had actually been reassurance for me. The apostle Peter says to leave our anxieties with God because he cares for us. Phyllis said the same with her life.

Remembering the changes yet to come for Phyllis, I took her hand. "Your family will be with you in your move. Every step of the way. That I can promise you."

Ever faithful, Phyllis looked out the window at the camellia and said, "I know."

Heavenly Father, let us not be anxious, knowing you care for us. Help us see the beauty surrounding us and the blessing yet to come. Amen.

Any overgrown, lopsided, misshapen shrubs in your garden?

Who has helped you see God's care for you?

Have you had an experience when you thought you were helping someone else, only to realize they were actually helping you?

"Especially for You, with Love."

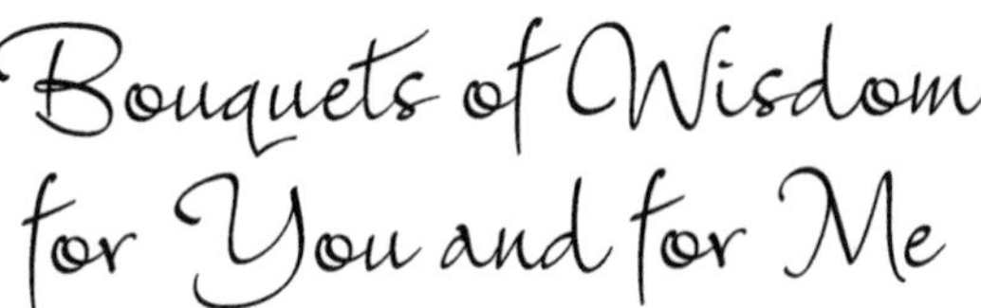

Bouquets of Wisdom for You and for Me

"The LORD your God is in your midst..."
- Zephaniah 3:17 (ESV)

Twenty-seven flowers, a couple weeds, and some ornamental grass, each a reminder of God's presence. Gathered together, they form a Bouquet of Wisdom, a divine gift.

God surrounds all of us with so many flowers. Some connect to special experiences, and these connections are not only beautiful and memorable but they help us better appreciate God in our midst—always. I need that assurance because so much in life is uncertain and I can worry about tomorrow. You might too.

While I was writing, my mother-in-law often talked about what her own bouquet might look like. She loved connecting flowers to stories about God's provision. How about you? What flowers has God placed in your Bouquet of Wisdom? Do you have stories about hollyhocks, marigolds, even a thistle? What flowers remind you of God and his love and care?

Yes, an exquisite bouquet! Handpicked by God and personally bestowed to each one of us with a card in the middle, "Especially for You, with Love."

Mighty and everlasting God, you remain in our midst. As we reflect back and look ahead, give us wisdom and understanding and an assurance in tomorrow. Amen.

My husband, Kurt

You continue to encourage and empower me with your love. I will be forever grateful that my stories are our stories. You are the kindest, most thoughtful person, and you continue to inspire not only me but all those around you.

My children, Kyle and Kevin

I love and adore you both. Being your mother has been my greatest joy. I treasure my time with each one of you and your families.

My daughters-in-law, Katie and Manoela

Dearest ladies, you are the most beautiful part of our family. I thank God for you both. I'm honored to share this life with you.

My grandchildren
Enzo, Austin, and Cameron

Our play dates are always the best. I love seeing the world through your eyes. You have taught me how to be in the moment, how to imagine the possibilities, and how to giggle at life's silliness. I'm a better for it.

My brother and sisters, David, Jill, Sara, and Gail

David, not only have I admired you, but I've learned from you. You're a great guy and a great brother! Jill and Sara and Gail, when I married Kurt, I had no idea how blessed I'd been with three sisters-in-love. I thank you for your love and support and the time we've had together in your mom's garden.

My Aunt Lorretta

Lorretta, I treasure our time together. You have grounded me with your wisdom, inspired me with your thoughtfulness and encouragement. I love you dearly.

My friend and colleague, Karen Rae

Your enthusiastic support of women has been a special blessing. Your belief in the possibilities has helped me take the smallest step in the biggest moments and helped me show up and shine. Thank you.

My friend and mentor, Michol Phillips

My dear Michol, you may be one chapter in the book, but your friendship spans many chapters. I appreciate your insight, your kindness and compassion. I always delight in our ability to solve the world's problems in a single cup of coffee.

My pastors and their wives,
Todd and Kim Roeske and Doug and Carole Iben

You all "walk the walk." You've helped me better understand what it means to be a follower of our Lord. Through your example, I've been able to see more clearly how God is truly in the details.

My boss, Jeff Ross and co-worker, Ayana Meissner

I love what I do and I love that I get to do it with you! Thank you for making it possible for me to write too.

My editor, Brenda Wilbee

I owe it all to you! You insisted on my best, refusing to give up on work that needed a lot of work! While I whined and complained, you encouraged and reassured, knowing that somewhere in the verbiage was a story waiting to be told. And you were right. I'm so very grateful!

Deanna Nowadnick is a motivational speaker and author of three books. Her writing has appeared in several print and online publications. When not writing, Deanna provides administrative support for The Planner's Edge, an investment advisory firm. Deanna lives in the Pacific Northwest with her husband Kurt.

CPSIA information can be obtained
at www.ICGtesting.com
Printed in the USA
JSHW010931250623
43581JS00005B/25